A Life Intertwined

"This is the story of my unique relationship with Raffles Hotel. I can say "There will always be a Raffles"

[signature]

Copyright © 2020 Raffles Hotel Singapore
Designed and produced by Epigram
Published by Raffles Hotel Singapore

National Library Board, Singapore
Cataloguing-in-Publication Data
Name:
Title: Danker, Leslie, 1939- | Raffles Hotel, publisher.
                 A life intertwined : reminiscences of an accidental Raffles historian
Description: / Leslie Danker.
Identifiers: Singapore : Raffles Hotel, 2020.
Subjects: OCN 1158894898 | ISBN 978-981-14-6303-7 (paperback)
                 LCSH: Danker, Leslie, 1939- | Raffles Hotel—Employees—
                 Anecdotes. | Raffles Hotel—History—Anecdotes. | Executives—
Classification: Singapore—Biography.
                 DDC 647.94092—dc23

Printed in Singapore
First edition, August 2020.
Second Printing, October 2021.

A LIFE INTERTWINED

Reminiscences of an Accidental Raffles Historian

LESLIE DANKER

RAFFLES

SINGAPORE

To my two beloved grandsons, Tyler and Kean, who have always been curious about Raffles Hotel Singapore. With this book they will have deeper knowledge of the hotel and one day, I hope they will be its ambassadors.

CONTENTS

Raffles Hotel Singapore
after its first restoration.

1

INTRODUCTION

I never set out to be any type of historian, let alone one for one of the most well-known luxury hotels in Singapore. Looking back, however, it seems that Raffles Hotel Singapore was always in my destiny. These pages tell of the roundabout way that I found my calling and of the tales and snippets that I have collected over the years about the hotel.

It was William Shakespeare who said, "There is a history in all men's lives." And I have been fortunate that mine includes the story, history and evolution of Raffles Hotel Singapore. To many, the building is a national landmark and an icon of our past; a place to bring out-of-town guests for a Singapore Sling or celebrate a special occasion.

To me, Raffles Hotel Singapore is a symbol of Singapore's collective memory and an integral part of our history. It was born in the nascent years of our founding, and has witnessed and weathered our country's trials, tribulations and triumphs: the colonial heyday, fall to the Japanese, fledgling nationhood and economic rise. It became such an institution among the colonial British living in newly founded

Singapore that it was simply known as "Raffles". To "Raffles" they would go for dinner, drinks or dancing—and even for the occasional roller skating party, fancy dress ball or movie.

On a more personal level, the hotel has been the barometer on which I have recorded a large part of my life. Over five decades, I have moved through the ranks and come to know it well, growing my enduring passion and interest in its rich and colourful history.

Skating dinners were a novel and popular form of entertainment, beginning in 1904 and running for about 15 years.

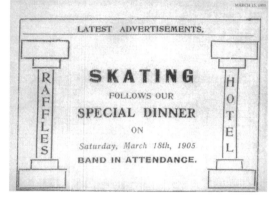

Raffles Hotel Singapore when it was completed in 1915.

The dining room
in the 1920s.

Raffles Hotel
Singapore in the
early 1900s.

Over the years, I have researched, collected and amassed (much to the chagrin of my wonderfully patient wife) a small library of clippings, notes and books that put together all the lesser-known stories and trivia of the goings-on at the hotel. Some of these you may have heard about—and others perhaps not. Scattered through these pages are some of the facts that I have unearthed. I hope that these stories will proffer some insight into my decades-long attachment (some might say obsession)—and personal history—with the enigmatic Raffles Hotel Singapore.

Rickshaws posing outside Raffles Hotel Singapore.

The hotel in the 1960s.

Façade of the hotel in 1991.

2

ALL ROADS LEAD TO
RAFFLES HOTEL SINGAPORE

The morning light bathes my face in its warm glow as I, and hundreds of other commuters, rise out of the subterranean warren of Dhoby Ghaut MRT station. As I make my way to the bus stop for the short ride to work, I am always struck by a conflicting sense of familiarity and strangeness. It seems that I have made this journey along Penang Road all my life, not just in my adult years working for the hotel, but all the way back to my boyhood. The route may be familiar, but so much has changed over the years. As I look upon the modern structures and restored buildings, my vision clouds with the vestigial traces of the old buildings, roads and activity of yore in the Dhoby Ghaut and Beach Road areas.

There, where a field once stood is a university campus, and where my childhood home used to stand are shopping malls. Gone are the shophouses and dirt roads, replaced by tarmac and developments of concrete, glass and steel.

My family—mother, father, three elder brothers, an elder sister,

My parents in their 20s in 1933.

myself and younger sister—lived for many years at 27 Penang Road in a three-bedroom semi-detached house. My father was an office administrator at the Public Works Department (today the PUB), my mother, a homemaker.

As I wait for my bus in the present day, I still see with my mind's eye the car workshops that lay across the street from our rows of houses. As a boy, I remember looking on in fascination at the mechanics in dark blue overalls tinkering with the squarish loaves of old model Fiats and Mercedes Benzes. Sometimes after school, I would spend hours just watching in wide-eyed and open-mouthed curiosity. Perhaps my gawping amused them, for after some time, these grime-covered and otherwise surly men got used to my presence and we became friends. For a time, I even entertained the idea of becoming a race car driver!

When I wasn't making a nuisance of myself, I would be in school. I enjoyed school and took part in many activities. Each day, I would take a 15-minute walk to St Joseph's Institution. From my home on Penang Road, I'd take a shortcut through the Presbyterian Church to get to Bras Basah Road and make my way to St Joseph's Institution via the Waterloo Street entrance. At lunch, I'd reverse my tracks and make the same journey home to eat a homecooked meal (although sometimes, as a treat, I'd eat from the famous Indian rojak stall along Waterloo Street). After lunch, I took the same route back to school for games and sports: catching, hockey, football or even practising the long jump. Then it was back home, where I would spend some time doing my homework before sitting down for dinner with my family. My father, a staunch Catholic, always insisted that the family pray together before we retired for bed. This was my routine and my route—back and forth—for all ten of my school-going years. And for the last five decades, I follow a similar journey from Penang Road to work as well. It's a wonder that I haven't made grooves in the roads!

These days, as my bus passes by my alma mater—now the Singapore Art Museum—I like to think about where my classes used to be and what I used to do in those carefree days. Whiling away my time hanging out with friends, having tea at the Catholic Centre, browsing books at one of the many bookshops along Bras Basah Road or going for a movie at the Cathay Cinema, which at that time was one of the fanciest buildings in Singapore.

Cathay Cinema in 1985.

New Lucky Store located on 37 Bras Basah Road in the 1960s (Indra Bahadur on the right).

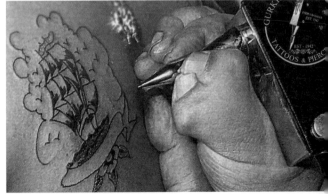

Indra Bahadur tattooing with his two thumbs.

Occasionally, I'd stop to peer curiously into one of the tattoo parlours, watching in fascination at the laborious, intricate (and to me, mildly shocking) process of ink being needled into skin. Set up in the 1950s by Indra Bahadur, a pioneer of Singapore's early tattoo scene, the shop, New Lucky Store, was better known as Johnny Two Thumbs, as Indra had a characteristic second thumb on his right hand. His legacy continues today—Gurkha Tattoo Family Pte Ltd, named in homage to its late founder, operates at Far East Plaza.

Sometimes, instead of walking, I would cycle up and down the streets along Beach Road, Connaught Drive and St Andrews Road, etching my own little roadmap of haunts and hang-out spots.

There is pleasant poignancy in this daily exercise in nostalgia. And it always amuses me that while I spent the whole of my growing-up years in the area, I never once set foot in Raffles Hotel Singapore until I turned 18. I had just finished school and was at loose ends about my next step in life. On a whim, I decided to ponder my future over a beer. Wandering somewhat nervously into the fan-cooled interior of the hotel, I made my way to the Long Bar, then situated within the ballroom (now the main driveway of the hotel). Ignorant of "the done thing", I ordered a draft beer instead of a Singapore Sling. Sinking into my rattan seat in the corner of the room, I sipped the frosty brew and mulled over my options. About an hour passed and—none the wiser for what I was about to do—I left. Little did I know that the hotel I was leaving would one day become a big part of my life.

1887—1899

In nearly a decade, the Sarkies brothers turned a humble ten-room bungalow into one of the grandest hotels in Singapore.

1887   The Sarkies brothers open Raffles Hotel Singapore in the European quarter. The ten-room bungalow overlooks the beach and the sea. This year coincides with the Golden Jubilee of Queen Victoria with pockets of celebratory and commemorative events across the British colonies.

The four Sarkies brothers: Aviet (far left), Arshak, Martin (seated) and Tigran (far right).

Raffles Hotel Singapore in 1887.

The statue of Sir Stamford Raffles (sculpted by Thomas Woolner) is unveiled at the Padang by the Governor of the Straits Settlement, Sir Frederick Weld, on Jubilee Day, 27 June. The statue is later moved to Victoria Theatre on the occasion of the 100-year anniversary of the founding of Singapore. The savvy Sarkies brothers capitalised on the historic moment and gave their new venture the name "Raffles Hotel".

As a young sailor, Joseph Conrad visited Singapore several times and his last visit in 1888 coincided with the opening of the hotel. It is believed that he walked from the Seamen's Mission a few blocks away to take a look at this new establishment. The description of a hostelry "as airy as a birdcage" in *The End of the Tether* is thought to be in reference to Raffles Hotel Singapore. In homage, a suite in the hotel is named after the author.

The unveiling of the Sir Stamford Raffles statue on Jubilee Day, 27 June 1887.

1888 Rudyard Kipling, as young journalist, visits Raffles Hotel Singapore when it is still in the process of being set up. His mixed review "Feed at the Raffles and sleep at the Hotel de L'Europe" (the more established competitor at the time) is cheekily edited by Tigran Sarkies to only tout the flattering first few words.

Rudyard Kipling.

1889– Over several years, the Sarkies brothers build up their hotel,
1899 leasing the land around the original Milton's Land and adding two wings on each side of the original structure.

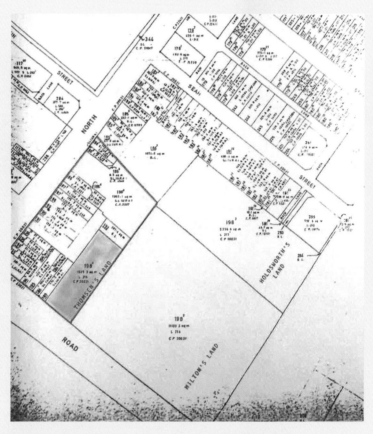

Area plan of Milton's Land.

1899 The main building of the hotel opens, replacing the old Beach House bungalow. Designed by Regent Alfred John Bidwell, the three-storey atrium is the epitome of luxury and sophistication.

Glass rooftop and dining room.

It is designed with glass tiles on the rooftop, which admits natural sunlight into the lobby. Built in grand Renaissance style, the Carrara marble-tiled ground floor dining room can fit 500—and becomes the place for balls and gala dinners. The hotel is also the first to have electric lights and fans powered by in-house generators. In the days of candlelight and kerosene lamps, so many incandescent and arc lights meant the ballroom must have shined like a beacon and glittered not only with light, but also with the who's who of society.

3

SCENES FROM MY CHILDHOOD

When I was a boy, Beach Road was truly near the beach. When I wasn't at school, playing sports or hanging out with friends at the Catholic Centre, I would enjoy some quiet time and cycle to the waterfront to watch the sea and daydream, do my homework or simply take long walks.

The original Satay Club was located off Beach Road near a bus terminal, which meant that in addition to smoke from grilling meat, there were fumes from rickety buses too. It was a favourite place to have dinner with my family on weekends after a movie at the Alhambra or Marlborough Theatre nearby. The Satay Club would move to a field between Prinsep Street and Dhoby Ghaut for a short time, before moving back to its original location. It would later move to Queen Elizabeth Walk (where the Esplanade now stands).

I was always active in school. I played football, represented my class in hockey (I was a goalkeeper) and was a long jumper. Most days after school were spent in the pursuit of one of these activities, typically in a large open field opposite St Joseph's Institution, where the Singapore Management University now stands.

Me in my school uniform (front row: seventh from right).

WELCOME TO RAFFLES

I jokingly call myself an accidental historian because my story with Raffles Hotel Singapore is something I stumbled into. It never crossed my mind that I would be in the hospitality industry, nor that I would ever be conferred the title of "historian"—trained in neither, I had spent the first 15 years of my working life in the social work sector, partly influenced by my Catholic upbringing. (Perhaps also due to the fact that I didn't quite make the cut for the Grand Prix nor the British colonial army; the former being too far out of reach and the latter never getting back to me on my application.)

The decade and a half I spent working with nursing homes, the elderly and the disabled are some of the most meaningful work I have ever done. I enjoyed interacting with people across different backgrounds, listening to their life stories, offering them help and connecting them with support and resources to improve their quality of life. But in 1972, I felt the need for a change.

My then-girlfriend and future wife, Theresa, supported me in my decision and I started looking for a job that would offer me similar opportunities to meet people and render help. I decided that the hotel sector might fit the bill. I was eager to learn new skills and was interested to see how I might apply my love for interacting with people from all walks of life to a new job.

The first hotel that came to mind was the hotel of my childhood. Fifteen years had passed since I had my single beer there and I had not revisited the hotel since. However, Raffles Hotel Singapore had always stood like a silent sentinel in the backdrop of my youth.

To this day, I don't know what possessed me to do what I did next.

My business cards over the years at the hotel as I assumed various roles.

With no plan in place, no experience to speak of, and not even a "help wanted" advertisement as a valid calling card, I walked up to the front desk one day and asked (somewhat naively and nervously) if I could speak to the manager about a job.

It was a wonder that I was not marched out of there. Instead, the front office turned me over to the general manager's secretary. I was instructed to take a seat in the administrative office and wait for the manager to return from his rounds of the hotel. And wait I did.

After what seemed like an eternity, a tall, energetic Caucasian gentleman bounded into the office, gave my hand a vigorous shake and asked me to take a seat. This was Mr Roberto Pregarz—a man I am forever indebted to, for just after a short introduction, he gave me my first job at Raffles Hotel Singapore as maintenance supervisor.

Mr Roberto Pregarz.

5

INTO THE FRAY

It turns out that while I had no hospitality qualifications to speak of, I had one skillset that was in high demand. I spoke English well. Mr Pregarz urgently needed someone to be able to communicate with guests as well as translate their requests to staff across the hotel. This was 1972, and at the time, many of the staff had no formal education and English-language skills. While they were good, loyal and hardworking, many of the back-of-house staff lacked formal hospitality training and the skills to communicate effectively with guests.

Excited as I was to score a job at the famous Raffles Hotel Singapore, my entry into the world of hospitality was rather anticlimactic. I had anticipated to work my way up, but not quite so literally. I didn't know what to expect, but a week later, I started my new job.

That first day, dressed in a crisp shirt and tie, I accompanied Mr Pregarz past the lobby, along the corridors and through a warren of doorways into the hidden belly of the hotel, my first-day jitters turned into a full-scale seismic event.

Working at ground level became my forte, even as I moved up the ranks.

I was introduced to a diverse crew of plumbers, painters, electricians and workmen. The group of Malay and Chinese gentlemen were all a decade or more older than myself. As maintenance supervisor, my job was to oversee their duties. Smiling nervously at my new team, I could feel sweat starting to trickle down my back, my confidence dissipating as quickly as my enthusiasm.

I did not know the first thing about plumbing, had never wielded a hammer in my life nor had an inkling of the intricacies of electrical wiring. Instead, I tapped on my people skills and channelled a little of that young boy who had harassed car technicians into first reluctant, then warm friendships. I asked questions, deferred to their expertise and soon grew a genuine interest in the various aspects of maintenance work. In fact, my colleagues were very generous with their advice and lessons, taking the time to impart their experience in various areas. Communicating in Malay, we'd spend our downtime teaching each other. I'd teach them a little English and they would show me how to unclog a toilet or fix faulty wiring. Thanks to them, I am quite the handyman today, if I do say so myself!

Some of this DIY knowledge came in handy during the first restoration.

The hotel's athletic team winning the Challenge Cup for the third consecutive year. I was their team manager.

When I was not at the back-of-house coordinating maintenance schedules with my team, I would be collating guest requests and managing complaints. Since I could speak English, I would also communicate with guests directly and ensure that my workmen colleagues understood their requests.

One aspect of the job was that I often had to accompany my colleagues to assignments. Remember, this was the 1970s. The Malayan Communist Party was in decline and there was a leadership struggle going on. The Malayan Emergency was still fresh in people's minds and Singapore was not as crime-free as it is today. Imagine if you were, say an elderly English lady, opening the door—only to see a burly workman in greasy-stained overalls wielding a wrench or some other intimidatingly heavy tool, speaking in an unknown tongue and making his way into the sanctuary of your room. Being able to explain the purpose of the visit, translate the guest's description of the defect, do a little service recovery and find out more about the particular guest's needs helped to smooth over potential misunderstandings. It was also an aspect of the job that allowed me to explore more of the hotel and interact more with its guests, a role that I enjoyed and continued to engage in for the whole of my career at Raffles Hotel Singapore.

Other staff members and I participating in a walk at the Padang on 27 August 1995.

My years as maintenance supervisor was a busy time. The hours were long and there was always something to be done. The hotel, while renowned for its beautiful architecture and historical value, was in need of ongoing repair. After all, the Grand Dame of Beach Road was 85 years old and showing her age. Down amid the pipes and plumbing, behind the walls among the wiring and up the roof of the hotel tending to leaks and creaks, I had a first-hand picture of the faults behind the façade.

Signs of the hotel's wear and tear leading to its much-needed facelift in 1989.

The hotel's main building under restoration on 18 May 1990.

Back of Palm Court Wing during the first restoration.

To me these age spots were part of the hotel's historic charm and lent depth to its fading beauty. Working in the back-end of the hotel did not blunt the allure for me. Instead, it heightened my growing interest in the hotel's storied past. Fixing up the hotel and exploring its many nooks and crannies revealed many secrets and gave intimate insight into how the original Raffles Hotel Singapore expanded and grew over time.

The team working on the pillars during the first restoration.

6

RAFFLES HOTEL SINGAPORE:
VERSION 1.0

My work as maintenance supervisor gave me unprecedented access to Raffles Hotel Singapore. Over the years, I observed many of its unique architectural features, and learnt about how the building grew and changed. These are some of the interesting details that I picked up.

SINGAPORE

Postcard of Raffles Hotel Singapore with the triangular pediment.

The pediment was originally triangular—as shown in the above postcard from 1910. Over the years, the triangular pediment was updated to its more modern rectangular shape to enhance its structural integrity. In these two images, you can also see the changes that were made over the years, such as an addition of a ground floor ballroom.

Rectangular pediment and ground floor ballroom.

One sign of the rapid growth of the hotel is a set of uneven pillars. These mismatched pillars came about when the hotel was expanded. One pillar was constructed in 1889, while the other was erected in 1894 when the Palm Court Wing was built. The rooms in this wing were constructed differently, with varying ceiling heights and details. It's an idiosyncratic quirk that marks the different phases of the hotel's "growth spurt" during its first flush of success.

These pillars are of uneven height because they were built at different times.

These two varying ceiling heights showcase the work of different architects at different times. The one in the foreground is straight, while the one in the background is slanted.

The old hotel lobby and mural in the late 1970s.

Before its first restoration in 1989, Raffles Hotel Singapore was in a rather sad state of disrepair. I recall the simple lobby, which was wood-panelled and open-aired, cooled only with ceiling fans. Above the reception desk hung a huge, distinctive mural by Gerard Henderson, a local artist. It depicted scenes of local life. Over the years, the ravages of time got to it and in the late 1970s, we realised it was being eaten up by termites. One day, during a lull between guest arrivals, we had to climb up a long ladder to smash the painting up, bit by bit, to dismantle it. The worn wall was smoothed out, replaced with planks and painted plain white.

Since there are not many reference photos of old Palm Court Suites, this illustration is based on my memory of the area.

The front entrances of the Palm Court Suites showing the rounded pillars that are halved by the wall.

One of the architectural quirks I noticed in my first years of the job is the way the columns along the corridor of Palm Court Suites are neatly dissected by the wall that separates the rooms from the veranda. In the early days of the hotel—likely before the advent of air-conditioning—an open-air sitting room fronted each of the suites with only a low parapet sectioning off the space from the public walkway.

Eventually, in the interest of privacy, security and a likely condescension to the weather, a wall was built to close off each room.

When I joined Raffles Hotel Singapore in 1972, keeping the old plumbing system going was one of the greatest challenges for the department. However, clogged toilets had nothing on this story that I unearthed about a bathroom mishap of major proportions. In 1904, before the days of water heaters and rain showers, baths in Raffles Hotel Singapore were taken "Asian" style, with large earthenware containers known as Shanghai Jars or "tongs". You were meant to scoop the water from these receptacles for your ablutions. One guest, mistaking it for a rather oddly shaped bathtub, contrived to immerse himself in the jar, and got stuck in the process. Luckily, a room attendant heard the cries for help. With the aid of a hammer and some deft strikes, the guest was extricated from his tubful of trouble.

THE MAKING OF AN ICON

1904—1921

With its beautiful architecture, famous eateries and bars as well as grand ballroom, Raffles Hotel Singapore became the social nexus for the who's who of Singapore.

1904 The Bras Basah Wing opens, catering to growing demand. The wing was converted from a row of horse stables previously owned by Harry Abrams (he moved his horse stables to Orchard Road). This expansion of 20 suites situated above a row of 11 shops makes Raffles Hotel Singapore the largest hotel in the Straits Settlement. Instead of wooden floorboards as featured in the other parts of the hotel, the veranda of this wing is decorated in richly patterned and coloured Minton tiles.

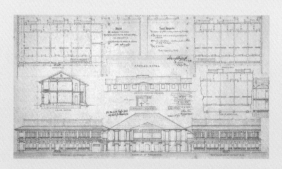

Plan of the proposed two wings and outbuilding for the hotel from 1889.

1910 The lobby is converted into a dining room, which hosts meals and dancing parties till the 1930s.

Main Dining Hall.

1915 The now-iconic Singapore Sling is invented by bartender Ngiam Tong Boon. Originally known as the "gin sling", the concoction of gin, cherry liqueur, dry curacao, grenadine and tropical juices, among other things, is a refreshing—if deceptively potent—alcoholic punch.

Ngiam Tong Boon, creator of the Singapore Sling.

Singapore Sling cocktail:

London Dry Gin
Bénédictine DOM
Cherry Liqueur
Dry Curacao
Pineapple Juice
Lime Juice
Grenadine Syrup
Bitters

Shake and pour over ice!

1915   All the major architectural works are completed. Raffles Hotel Singapore is set to enter the roaring '20s to be *the* place to see and be seen.

Raffles Hotel Singapore in 1910.

1920 Singapore's early days of being a travel destination begins with many European tourists arriving by ship via the Suez Canal. Ships anchor in the outer waters and are ferried in smaller boats to Johnston's Pier. From there, guests make their way to their hotels. Catering to travellers, the Sarkies start the Raffles Motor Garage, a limousine service with 17 British and French cars. Car repairs, rentals and garage services are also available.

Raffles Motor Garage.

1921 The Ballroom opens and hosts many vibrant evenings all the way till the 1930s. Fancy dress balls, dinner, tea dances, cabaret shows and even clattering roller-skating parties spill over into the lobby. During many of these parties, the rich and famous make merry to the jaunty tunes played by the Dan Hopkins band under the baton of the said director.

The Ballroom in the 1920s.

The Dan Hopkins band.

The annual Fancy Dress Ball was the highlight of the social calendar.

Ms Jill Hill, an Australian who studied classical dancing in Berlin and was a renowned dance teacher, opens the Jill Hill Dance Studio on the ground floor of the Bras Basah Wing and teaches modern dance.

7

FROM CISTERNS
TO KITCHENS

For me, 1975 was a memorable year. That year, I married my wife, Theresa, after a five-year courtship. Over all the years of our marriage, my dear Theresa has been very understanding of my long working hours—which became even more protracted as my career at Raffles Hotel Singapore reached its next milestone.

Having shaped up the maintenance team and trained them sufficiently to attend to needs at the back-of-house, Mr Pregarz decided it was time for me to "handle the other end of the food chain". Quite literally, too.

This took the form of a promotion of sorts to food and beverage (F&B) supervisor. In this role I oversaw the hotel's eating establishments running at the time: the Tiffin Room, the Elizabethan Grill, the Palm Court Restaurant and the Main Ballroom. This included supervising the kitchens, managing waitstaff, developing menus with the chefs, scheduling work rosters and human resources.

While the environment changed, much of the work remained the same. I still had to act as interpreter between guests and staff, many of whom, like their counterparts in the maintenance department, did not speak English well. And unlike waitstaff today, they had undergone little service training, if at all. This meant I reprised my role as the go-between, smoothing over miscommunications and language barriers.

I patrolled the dining room, stepping in to translate requests and ensure that guests had their needs met. In those days, it was common for guests to dine al fresco at Palm Court, weather permitting. One local superstition was to hang out chillies to ward off the rain. But such efforts could not always be relied upon to deter Mother Nature and many a time, the rain would fall nevertheless, sometimes mid-meal. There would be an ensuing frenzy as diners dashed to take cover even as waiters carried the tables towards shelter with practised skill.

Beyond this, there were also catering assignments and banquets to manage. Since Rudyard Kipling's double-edged compliment in the 1888 review ("Feed at the Raffles and sleep at the Hotel de L'Europe"), the hotel had certainly stepped up on the former and continued to build up its F&B offerings to become one of the most elegant of dining establishments.

These catering affairs had the complexity and precision of a military drill parade with hundreds of moving parts and requests—especially if it involved dignitaries or took place outside the hotel. One of these catered dinners memorably took place at the Istana (Malay for "palace"), the official residence and office of the president of Singapore.

I had the unlikely challenge of transporting the Raffles Grill's distinct silver dinner wagon into the event hall. I could not very well ask the waiters, who were all in their 50s and 60s to do so. So, with youthful bravado I hoisted the heavy-wheeled serving trolley (which weighed about 40kg), delicate curved legs and all, down a series of wide steps into the venue. To this day, I don't know how I managed to do so without rolling down those steps head over tea kettle and denting the stately antique in the process. What a disaster it would have been!

Hotel staff with a silver beef wagon in 1981.

Legend has it that this silver dinner wagon survived World War II. In the hours just before the Japanese invasion of Singapore, the hotel staff buried it and a collection of silverware in a secret location on the grounds. After the war, these were dug up, polished and put back into commission. It makes me shudder to think that this service wagon survived the Japanese Occupation, only to be damaged in an ignominious trundle down presidential stairs at the hands of a multi-tasking F&B manager!

The stately silver wagon has presided over many elegant meals.

The multi-tasking also included managing the Malayan Night, a cultural show held in the Raffles Ballroom. The evening consisted of a buffet dinner and cultural dance performances from across Asia.

Malayan Night brochures.

The night's entertainment included a lion or a Chinese fan dance, Malay joget tari payong (an umbrella dance) and Keralan kathakali dance with elaborate costumes and masks. The finale—and audience favourite—was the Filipino tinikling, a dexterous hopping dance where one had to step into and out of two bamboo poles that were clapped together in rhythm.

Brave audience members would volunteer to try it out, no doubt buoyed by the music, good food and high spirits. In all my years managing the night, only one person took a misstep, getting her foot trapped between the fast-moving poles. Fortunately, she was not hurt and had a memorable tale to bring home with her.

WINDS OF CHANGE

1930—1953

Raffles Hotel Singapore witnessed more than gaiety and grand times having survived the Great Depression as well as World War II. In the post-war years, it quickly rose to greater heights of glamour.

1930s The Great Depression strikes its blow. The global economy stagnates and tourist numbers fall, severely affecting the hotel trade. The glamorous parties, dinners and fêtes at Raffles dwindle. The downturn coincides with the Sarkies' ill-timed acquisition of new hotels and the upgrading of existing ones, sinking the firm into a deep financial hole. With the death of Arshak—the last of the living Sarkies brothers—in 1931, the company collapses and is declared insolvent in one of the largest bankruptcy cases of the time. Thanks to its reputation and historical significance, the hotel is kept. Raffles Hotel Limited is formed and new management is brought in to upgrade the hotel. By the late 1930s, fortunes revive, and Raffles Hotel Singapore is once again hosting celebrities, writers and socialites. But it was not to last...

1941 One of the first privately owned bomb shelters in Singapore is built in the hotel by its own engineering staff. Under the direction of Mr J.F. James, five motor garages are reinforced with brick on all sides and a 15cm-thick concrete roof. It can shelter 120 guests.

The garage, which was converted into a bomb shelter, being demolished.

"This garage-bomb shelter was still in use when I joined the hotel and I used to park my car in it! It was later demolished during the first restoration of the hotel."

This is the extent of the preparedness, however. While whispers of war and an imminent Japanese invasion bandied about, the British remain confident that an attack will not happen. There is even a dinner and dance in January 1942 at Raffles Hotel Singapore, which culminates in a song that includes the line: "there will always be a Singapore".

RAFFLES HOTEL

TO-NIGHT
SPECIAL DINNER & DANCE
from 7pm to 10pm

ligula quis orci Np la eget.   Lorem ipsum dolor

THE HIGHLANDER

Lorem ipsum dolor sit amet consectetur adipiscing elit Mauris vulputate at ipsum non suscipit Fusce sed venenatis orci Suspendisse finibus metus sit amet condimentum ultricies mi sapien tempor orci eu lobortis est tellus a nisi Nullam non diam tristique faucibus nisl vitae fermentum libero Cras dapibus euismod justo vel ullamcorper lectus posuere quis Duis ullamcorper leo a viverra blandit enim ante facilisis ligula eu accumsan lectus ligula quis orci Nulla eget ante finibus sollicitudin nisi ut euismod tortor Curabitur non ex a leo eleifend tempus Donec aliquet vestibulum justo vel vehicula Aliquam non eleifend turpis Vivamus varius ipsum arcu ut lobortis lectus posuere et Vivamus at tempor augue nec maximus tellus Vestibulum ante ipsum primis in faucibus orci luctus et ultrices posuere cubilia Curae Nunc rhoncus maximus ligula

Lorem ipsum dolor sit amet consectetur adipiscing elit Mauris vulputate at ipsum non suscipit Fusce sed venenatis orci Suspendisse finibus metus sit amet condimentum ultricies mi sapien tempor orci eu lobortis est tellus a nisi Nullam non diam tristique faucibus nisl vitae fermentum libero Cras dapibus euismod justo vel ullamcorper lectus posuere quis Duis ullamcorper leo a viverra blandit enim ante facilisis ligula eu accumsan lectus ligula quis orci Nulla eget ante finibus sollicitudin nisi ut euismod tortor Curabitur non ex a leo eleifend tempus Donec aliquet vestibulum justo vel vehicula Aliquam non eleifend turpis Vivamus varius ipsum arcu ut lobortis lectus posuere et Vivamus at tempor augue nec maximus tellus Vestibulum ante ipsum primis in faucibus orci luctus et ultrices posuere cubilia Curae Nunc rhoncus maximus ligula

Lorem ipsum dolor sit amet consectetur adipiscing elit Mauris vulputate at ipsum non suscipit Fusce sed venenatis orci Suspendisse finibus metus sit amet condimentum ultricies mi sapien tempor orci eu lobortis est tellus a nisi Nullam non diam tristique faucibus nisl vitae fermentum libero Cras dapibus euismod justo vel ullamcorper lectus posuere quis Duis ullamcorper leo a viverra blandit enim ante facilisis ligula eu accumsan lectus ligula quis orci Nulla eget ante finibus sollicitudin nisi ut euismod tortor Curabitur non ex a leo eleifend tempus Donec aliquet vestibulum justo vel vehicula Aliquam non eleifend turpis Vivamus varius ipsum arcu ut lobortis lectus posuere et Vivamus at tempor augue nec maximus tellus Vestibulum

Lorem ipsum dolor sit amet consectetur adipiscing elit Mauris vulputate at ipsum non suscipit Fusce sed venenatis orci Suspendisse finibus metus sit amet condimentum ultricies mi sapien tempor orci eu lobortis est tellus a nisi Nullam non diam tristique faucibus nisl vitae fermentum libero Cras dapibus euismod justo vel ullamcorper lectus posuere quis Duis ullamcorper leo a viverra blandit enim ante facilisis ligula eu accumsan lectus ligula quis orci Nulla eget ante finibus sollicitudin nisi ut euismod tortor Curabitur non ex a leo eleifend tempus Donec aliquet vestibulum justo vel vehicula Aliquam non eleifend turpis Vivamus varius ipsum arcu ut lobortis lectus posuere et Vivamus at tempor augue nec maximus tellus Vestibulum ante ipsum primis in

But as history tells us, Singapore falls a month later and the Japanese army moves their officers and civilian administrators into the hotel, which is renamed Synonan Ryokan (or "Light of the South Hotel").

"During the Japanese bombing of Singapore, much of the hotel was spared, however, a bomb that destroyed the laundry in the back of the hotel sadly killed an Indian porter. I once told the history of the hotel and its time during the war to a British Indian couple; they revealed that the poor man was one of their relatives."

THE WAR YEARS

1942—1945

I was only a toddler during the Japanese Occupation of Singapore, so I don't remember much, although I faintly recall seeing the Japanese army march past my house with British and Australian prisoners of war. At the time, my family lived in a terraced house in the government quarters along Bukit Timah Road just down the street from the then Kandang Kerbau Hospital. During the war, we were told to build a bomb shelter in our backyard—essentially a trench in the ground. The hole was about 1.2m deep with planks and dirt for a rough ceiling. When the sirens went off, my family of seven would rush into it, forcing ourselves into the cramped and stuffy hole, praying fervently for God's protection. Around us, there would be a cacophony of noise whooshing, shouting, rumbles and crying. Even more eerie were the quieter sounds—tense silences, mysterious rustlings and most ominous of all, the faint whistling that preceded the bone-jarring impact of a bomb hitting its mark. Our home was lucky to have been spared, but a neighbouring house was not as fortunate and suffered some damage from a nearby bomb. Thankfully, no one was harmed.

While our backyard served as a bomb shelter, large parts of the front yard were used to grow tapioca to supplement the scant war rations. As Eurasians, we had the ironic fortune to feel safer as we were viewed as less of a threat than people of Chinese descent. With six young children to care for, we were also lucky that my father kept his job in the Public Works Department—which meant we could still make ends meet, albeit barely—and saw us safely through to the end of the war.

1947   In the post-war years, glamour returns to Raffles Hotel Singapore—a significant part of it in the form of Australian concert pianist turned fashion designer Doris Geddes, who sets up The Little Shop, selling European-made handbags and stylish cocktail dresses. Located where the East India Rooms now stand, the shop was a fixture for over three decades. It clothed visiting dignitaries, local socialites and even celebrities, including Elizabeth Taylor.

Elizabeth Taylor in Singapore dressed in a gown designed by Doris Geddes, 1957.

Glamorous Mrs Geddes.

"When I got to meet her in the late 1970s, Mrs Geddes was a tour de force and I had many opportunities in my career to experience her sharp tongue and larger-than-life personality. Most of her tirades began with, 'Young man! Sit down!' But beneath the diva and her grievances about leaks and plumbing was a rather sweet and feisty lady who really wanted to wax nostalgic about her glory days dressing royalty and hobnobbing with socialites."

"No longer buoyed by her charisma and style, The Little Shop shuttered several years after Mrs Geddes passed away in the mid 1970s. During the auction of the store's remaining treasures, I bought two porclelain cats. Whenever I look at them, I almost expect to hear Mrs Geddes' strident voice call out to me."

1953   The Grill Room is renamed the Elizabethan Grill in honour of the Queen's coronation. This revamp is the first of many. In 1991, after the first restoration, the English-style grill, with its mock fireplace, is wholly restored and becomes the Raffles Grill.

The wood-panelled Elizabethan Grill.

Raffles Grill.

Today, La Dame de Pic Raffles takes its place and continues the tradition of fine dining in elegant settings.

Interior of the beautifully designed La Dame de Pic by the three-Michelin-star chef Anne-Sophie Pic.

One of the many alcoves at La Dame de Pic that offers guests an intimate dining experience.

TALES FROM
THE BAR(S)

Bar stories abound at Raffles Hotel Singapore, home to the iconic Long Bar, the Bar and Billiard Room, as well as the old Tiger's Tavern. The Tavern (which operated from 1979 to 1989 and was located at Mrs Geddes' former shop) was a cabin-like pub, decked in wooden walls and floors, tiger motifs and rifles carved from wood. The hotel's carpenters had done such an impressive job with them that they looked real. In fact, the story goes that one was actually stolen. The light-fingered gentleman even had the audacity to return with it asking for a replacement as the one he had shoplifted was not working!

As for the Long Bar, the Raffles Hotel Singapore institution has moved with the times in more ways than one. The bar counter was first located in the far right end of the Ballroom, then on the ground floor where the driveway now stands along Beach Road. This meant that guests had to walk through the Ballroom for their Singapore Slings. In 1974, I was involved in moving the bar to the left side of the Ballroom, nearer to the entrance, which made it more convenient for

Long Bar in
the 1980s,
with me
seated in the
centre.

Tiger's
Tavern in
1979.

Long Bar Steakhouse in 1991.

The refreshed Long Bar in 1991.

cocktail hour. I remember that the new bar counter was made by the ever-handy carpenters of the hotel, and we roped in the F&B staff to move crates of glasses and bottles to the new location. Among some of these waitstaff and bartenders were descendants of Singapore Sling creator Mr Ngiam Tong Boon, a fact that was made clear to me when I called out "Ngiam!", looking for Robert Ngiam (who was a waiter), and several of them raised their hands in reply.

As the place for Singapore Slings, the Long Bar has seen its fair share of Sling aficionados. I too experienced a quintet of them in 1978—an Englishman, Welshman, a Scot and two Australians—who consumed a remarkable 131 Singapore Slings in the span of two hours!

The spiral staircase and swaying fans have become iconic features of the Long Bar.

8

ANIMAL STORIES

World travellers and celebrities were not the only guests at Raffles Hotel Singapore. Back when Singapore was less urbanised and home to rubber plantations and fruit orchards, it was not uncommon to see critters and creatures of varying sizes and varieties make their way into homes and buildings. Some, even visited the hotel—perhaps in an attempt to partake of a Singapore Sling.

THE ORIGINAL TIGER TALE

In 1902, a Bengal tiger, a supposed escapee from a nearby circus, made its way to the Bar and Billiard Room one morning. Mr Charles McGowan Phillips, principal of the neighbouring Raffles Institution, was roused from his bed by the hotel staff. Clad in pyjamas and armed with his Lee-Enfield rifle, he stalked the tiger, which was hiding under the elevated floor of the bar. The first three shots missed, but the fourth found its mark. The tiger was 2.3m long and about a metre high.

A SERPENT AT DAWN

Just several months after the alarming tiger shoot, a gardener encountered a large python while watering the potted palms outside the veranda of the dining hall. Mistaking the dark coiled mass for an overcoat misplaced by a guest, the gardener reached out for it, only to be terrified out of his wits as the 4.5m snake unwound itself. Gathering several of his compatriots and a number of bamboo poles, the snake was captured alive and was transported to the Botanic Gardens where it lived out its remaining days.

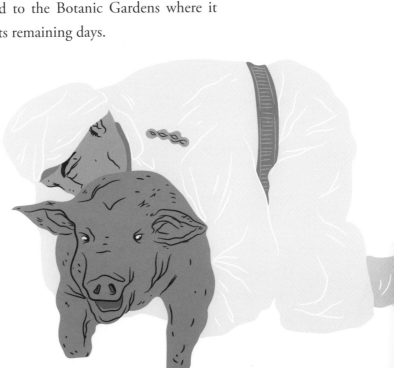

THE JAGA, THE BOAR AND THE PIG

A portly jaga (watchman) found unlikely hero status when he—on not one, but two occasions—tackled animal invaders. Once, a wild boar was found wandering outside the Bar and Billiard Room. Much to the amusement of guests, the jaga (decked in his regalia: turban, white coat, yellow sash and all) wrestled the muscular animal to the ground, only to lose his hold on it. Grabbing a stick, he charged the animal, chasing if off the grounds. The scenario repeated itself a year later when a pig dashed into the hotel and ran amok in the flowerbeds. Re-deploying his porcine combat techniques, the jaga chased down the squealing intruder, ending in its neat capture.

THE RETURN OF THE TIGER

Thankfully for me, I never had to hunt tigers, capture snakes or wrestle pigs in my time. But I did get to experience my own tiger tale. In February 1986, the hotel partnered with the Chipperfield Circus to commemorate the year of the tiger. Seta, a 113kg Bengal tiger, was brought to the Bar and Billiard Room where she serenely wandered the room and lay on the billiard table as reporters and photographers chronicled the event.

CHARMS OF THE SNAKE

More snakes would become part of Raffles Hotel Singapore's animal lore. For almost a decade, from the 1970s to 1980s, a snake charmer would perform at the front of the hotel, making a living from playing his flute-like naskar to entice his snake into a languid dance.

MARTIN THE MONKEY

I also got to meet a cheeky monkey one day in 1993, when the nimble fellow introduced himself to astonished guests. Swinging from tree to tree in the lush garden underneath the first floor suites, "Martin" the monkey provided the morning's entertainment and showcased the tropical wildlife to our out-of-town guests.

ON THE FRONT LINES

The year was 1980. After five years working in F&B, Mr Pregarz decided it was time for another change and for me to take on more responsibility as front office manager. It was an evolution of what I had been doing all along, with the added responsibility of being more customer-facing. It was a challenge I was all too happy to undertake.

Little did I expect just how big that challenge would be. It was an "everything but the kitchen sink" type of job, except that the kitchens happened to be involved too. It meant tending to and documenting guest requests and complaints, monitoring and managing hotel security, coordinating with all the hotel departments such as housekeeping, maintenance and F&B. Importantly, it also comprised overseeing reservations and guest registrations.

With hotel occupancy at its height in the 1980s, managing reservations became one of my biggest jobs. Unlike today where we have sophisticated computer systems that make the work seamless and convenient, everything was very manual back then. Each guest registration was recorded into giant ledgers, the details painstakingly duplicated by hand for the various departments.

Guests who made hotel reservations in advance would have to wait as we flipped through old records to find the right information. Behind the reception desk was a wall of pigeonholes for keys with cards labelled with the name of the occupying guest. Sorting through the cards, we could tell when the current guest was checking out and when the next one was arriving.

Working in the Front Office Department.

The manual registration system, in particular, made it difficult to ascertain the hotel's occupancy levels. Once, I remember being overbooked and a British guest had to be turned away. The lady was distraught at not being able to stay at the hotel—it was a dream of hers. I arranged for her stay at another hotel, with costs borne by the hotel, and invited her back for lunch the next day.

At the time, even the phones were still on a switchboard system, and the lift was a caged affair with a folding latticed door. On the rare occasions that it got stuck, one of the staff (or myself) had to crawl under the landing of the first floor and use a crank to turn a gear and bring the lift home to the ground level.

Though not all of the hotel's operations were modernised in the 1980s, Raffles Hotel Singapore kept up her impeccable standards and service levels through the hard work and passion of all those who worked there. The needs of guests always came first and were anticipated. The hotel retained its reputation for discreet luxury and comfort.

Looking back at the improvements that have been made since then, from computer systems, professional service training and operating procedures, I am proud of how much the hotel has grown from strength to strength, rising to become one of the top hotels in the world not just for its historical charm but its first-class service.

Life at the front desk meant long hours, multiple responsibilities and working an overnight shift on the weekend. I'd clock in for duty on Saturday afternoon and knock off on Sunday afternoon. Though the job had its challenges, I enjoyed the privilege of tending to guest's needs and seeing that the hotel's operations ticked along.

There were also some perks. These overnight shifts meant that I had the unusual pleasure of sleeping in any of the available suites. At 1am, after making sure the gate in front of the hotel was secure, I would check on the status of our rooms and select one that was not being occupied. Apart from enjoying the luxury of the room, a benefit I was often too tired to appreciate, it also meant that I could do quick spot checks of each suite and take note of maintenance issues.

These late shifts were interesting in their own way. For one, I would come to know which of our guests were night owls. As the front entrance of the hotel was secured at midnight, late-coming carousers would have to rattle the collapsible gate to alert the front desk to be let in.

It was during this time in the late '80s that I began to invest more time into researching the hotel, its history and stories. Even more so after 1987 when the hotel was gazetted as a national historical monument. Guests often asked about the hotel and I felt it was only professional to be able to provide the information. It was heartening to see people so interested in Raffles Hotel Singapore and its rich and colourful past. It was my privilege to be able to share her story with the world.

10

CELEBRITY SIGHTINGS

Raffles Hotel Singapore's fame has lasted for many decades, long before it was gazetted as a historical icon. A beacon of Singapore's social scene for years, the hotel has wined, dined and roomed countless celebrities, writers, politicians and royalty. In my time working here, I have had the honour of meeting many famous people, almost too many to count.

Filming at the hotel for the movie *Saint Jack*, late 1970s.

Filming the TV series *Tenko* at the hotel's side entrance during the early 1980s.

The Raffles Hall of Fame—I've had the privilege of meeting many of the celebrities on this wall.

The fact that the hotel was often used as a setting for movies added to the star sightings. In the late 1980s, General Manager Mr Pregarz jokingly called me "movie director" and directed all requests to me. Here, in no particular order are some of my favourite celebrity sightings.

DONNY AND MARIE OSMOND
The siblings were very cheerful and friendly, chatting with me for several minutes after the photo was taken.

BEN GAZZARA

I first met the actor when he was in Singapore filming *Saint Jack*, the controversial movie that was banned here for several years. Mr Gazzara would visit Singapore several more times and what touched me was that he would make it a point to look me up every time he was in town.

DIONNE WARWICK

I spotted her in the hotel lobby and approached her for a photo. The gentleman she was with forbade me from standing next to her for the shot, so in this photo, he is standing between me and the famous singer. I learnt later that he was her bodyguard.

JACKIE CHAN

The mega movie star is one of the friendliest and most approachable celebrities that I have met and a frequent guest at Raffles Hotel Singapore. Always jovial and entertaining, Mr Chan never fails to call out, "Mr Leslie!" when he sees me.

JACK LORD

Of *Hawaii Five-O* fame, he was filming for the episode titled, "The Year of the Horse". This episode included an exciting car chase scene that took place at the entrance of the hotel carpark.

BRUCE BOXLEITNER

He was filming the 1986 movie *Passion Flower* on location at the hotel. Tall, gentlemanly and obliging, he was very friendly during the photo taking.

MICHAEL JACKSON

The King of Pop was in Singapore in 1993 as part of his Dangerous Tour. I had the privilege of meeting him and observed that he is very soft spoken in person, contrary to his loud and dynamic stage personality.

11

A TIME FOR RENEWAL

Armed with my knowledge of the hotel, my role at the front desk soon included taking guests on tours of the hotel. One day, in 1987, I was asked to take a very special visitor around, Mr Richard Helfer, the newly appointed head of Raffles Hotel Singapore Pte Ltd, then the new holding company for the hotel. He was to be given a comprehensive tour of the hotel, peeling paint, odd restoration quirks and all.

Mr Helfer's job and vision was to restore the ageing hotel to her former grandeur and bring her back to its glory days in 1915 when Raffles Hotel Singapore was at its height of beauty and elegance. The idea excited me, but there was also the ominous thought: if the hotel closed for several years for extensive restoration, what would happen to me and the rest of the staff? For many, it marked an opportune time to retire, while others made plans to seek jobs elsewhere. I was at a loss—at almost 50 years old and with two daughters still in school, I wondered where I would end up.

These thoughts weighed on me for several weeks, flitting through my thoughts as I went about my day showing consultants, architects and engineers around the hotel. Then an amazing thing happened— Mr Helfer pulled me aside one day and asked if I wanted to stay on. My in-depth knowledge of the hotel would come in handy during the restoration. The eclectic career that spanned the maintenance department to the front desk came in handy after all. This new opportunity lent a bittersweet touch to the days leading up to the hotel's closure at midnight on 15 March 1989. My wonderful colleagues were happy for me, and all of them promised to visit when the hotel reopened.

The staff and me on 15 March 1989, the last day before the hotel closed for restorations.

EVER ONWARDS, EVER UPWARDS

1987—2020

Raffles Hotel Singapore is a local icon that embodies the spirit of reinvention that is rooted in tradition, culture and history.

1987 Raffles Hotel Singapore is designated a national monument.

Plaque commemorating the status of national monument.

1989   The hotel closes on 15 March for a multi-million dollar restoration that would see it return to its former glory in 1915, its benchmark year.

Artisan working on the pillars.

Hotel façade under restoration.

1991   After two-years of intensive work, Raffles Hotel Singapore re-opens on 16 September to much fanfare.

• 1993   The tradition of the New Year's Eve Gala Ball at the Raffles Hotel Singapore lobby is revived.

New Year's Eve Ball in the 1990s.

• 1996   The Bras Basah Wing of Raffles Hotel Singapore is re-established as Raffles Inc. The wing houses 18 commodious State Rooms.

Bras Basah Wing.

2007   Raffles Hotel Singapore celebrates her 120th birthday in splendid style with a grand Gala Reception on 16 September. Minister Mentor Lee Kuan Yew graces the event as guest of honour.

Lee Kuan Yew kicking off the birthday bash.

2015   The Singapore Sling marks its centennial anniversary. To commemorate the event, a bespoke gin, Raffles 1915, is created in partnership with Sipsmith. Sam Galsworthy, co-founder of Sipsmith, happens to be a direct descendant of Sir Stamford Raffles.

12

EMPLOYEE 10001:
FRESH STARTS AND FINDS

My new job began the very next day, on 16 March 1989. As employee number one, my first job was to sort through the hotel's furnishings and other items, categorise them for storage, showcase or disposal. Some historic pieces were identified for careful restoration and these were also marked with a brass plate noting it as a "Raffles Original". It took me six months to sort through the thousands of items, many of them worn beyond repair.

My employee identification card showing that I was the first staff member in this new chapter of the hotel's history.

When I was not taking stock of the hotel's furnishings and items, I would be in the site office. There, I would file and track the architecture and engineering plans. But most exciting of all was taking progress photos of the demolition, excavation and construction work. Kitted out in a hard hat and rubber boots, armed with my camera and fuelled with overwhelming curiosity, I felt like an intrepid archaeologist digging for buried treasure!

By then, I had worked at the hotel for 17 years and had spent much of that time acquiring knowledge about her history. This restoration gave me the literal chance to unearth a myriad of hidden stories, treasures and a true-to-life skeleton! As the construction crew chipped away at the additions, lowered false ceilings, dividing walls and other structures that had been added over the years, Raffles Hotel Singapore revealed her secrets.

I discovered hundreds of pottery shards in an old kitchen dump. One of these bore the distinctive flourish of the Sarkies crest. The shard rests today in the Raffles Museum.

Sarkies crest.

The old worn marble floor of the Main Building was removed. The once-glossy Carrara marble, defaced by roller skating parties and decades of human traffic, was found to have been laid over terracotta tiles. These were the foundation of the original Beach House, the bungalow that the Sarkies leased and turned into Raffles Hotel Singapore. During the first restoration when the Carrara marble flooring was removed, I discovered that sea sand was under the marble flooring. The sea was at the front of the hotel at that time. I collected that sand in a tube.

Container of sea sand I collected during the hotel's first restoration.

Horse carriages at the front of the hotel in the late 1800s.

At the back of the Palm Court Wing, workers were amazed to find the buried remains of an adult horse. The bones lay among a scattering of horseshoes and earthenware bottles. This discovery harks to the time when the Harry Abrams Stables formed part of the hotel site.

Horse stables owned by Harry Abrams were located at the Brash Basah Wing in the late 1800s. Here's what the wing looks like today.

The famous Bar and Billiard Room, site of the famous tiger hunt, had been converted into guest rooms in 1917. During the careful restoration of this room, layers of plaster and paint were removed to reveal a worn, but unmistakable "RH" monogram.

One of the most challenging restorations was that of the cast-iron portico. The original structure adorned the entrance of the hotel from 1913 to 1919 before it was torn down to construct the Ballroom. Eagle-eyed restorers found a remaining part of the original metalwork hidden in a corner of the roof. Microfilms of the design were traced to Scotland and the whole structure was faithfully replicated by specialists, Robinson Iron, in Alabama, USA.

And even as the layers of time and age were being peeled way, fresh new life was being breathed and built back into Raffles Hotel Singapore. Decorative plasterwork, much of which had been unthinkingly covered up by paint and plaster, or damaged by time and grime, were once again remodelled to their former intricate beauty.

Restored cast-iron portico.

Outdoor space at Doc Cheng's.

A new skylight bathed the smooth gleaming marble floors and pure white walls in warm rays. Rooms were redecorated to offer cosy luxury, furnished with Oriental carpets, warm woods, fine leather and silky linens. The Bar and Billiard Room and Long Bar were resurrected, as was the Tiffin Room, in addition to new dining concepts such as the Raffles Grill, Doc Cheng's and Ah Teng's Bakery.

When the hotel opened in 1991 to a grand fête on par with those held in its heyday, my heart burst with pride. As much as I loved Raffles Hotel Singapore with her patina of faded elegance, I loved this restored version of her just as well. It felt like a rare privilege for someone like me. I had always been enamoured with her past and what a treat it was to see Raffles Hotel Singapore returned to those glory days that I have read so much about.

Ah Teng's Bakery.

Complementing this "return to 1915" was an improvement on the other end of the time spectrum: the embrace of new technology, enhanced systems, and the creation of departments and specialised roles. This was Raffles Hotel Singapore at her restored and renewed best.

As for me, I became chief information officer for three years before taking on the role of guest relations manager and then becoming a training manager. In 2004, I was made resident historian—possibly the first in-house hotel historian in Singapore, a job I deeply enjoy. My role consists of meet-and-greets with guests over breakfast and ascertaining their interest in going on a history tour of the hotel. Some days these take the form of personalised sessions with just one or two guests, while some "history lessons" are done with larger groups. As a resident historian, I undertake all media interviews like those from BBC and other European and Asian outlets.

It has given me the chance to become fast friends with some of our regular hotel guests, or "residents", as we call them at Raffles Hotel Singapore. They always show such a keen interest in the stories I have to tell, and it is always a pleasure to regale them with these over breakfast, a cup of tea or a Singapore Sling.

Fountain at Palm Garden.

Façade of restored Raffles Hotel Singapore in 2019, after its second restoration.

13

A NEW CHAPTER

Today, I have the joy of seeing Raffles Hotel Singapore undergo its second restoration, 28 years after its first. This second restoration is so meaningful to me as it brings the hotel back to its roots, while it also elevates and builds on its legacy of hospitality and luxury.

Starting in 2017 and finishing in 2019, this sensitive restoration of the hotel's historical features is coupled with discreet modern updates and added luxury touches that breathe new life into Raffles Hotel Singapore once again. While I have a much less active role this time in the works, it is truly gratifying to know that the Grand Dame of Beach Road will once again be primed for her next phase of life.

As the hotel turns the page to a new beginning, I have been grooming a new generation of Raffles historians and developing new history tours for guests. Going on site visits a few times a week gives me an unparalleled opportunity to see the work that is being done. Even after all these years, the hotel still has so many secrets to reveal. On one of these weekly site walks in 2018, I noticed that the workmen had

A discovery overhead, a second ceiling above the Writers Bar and Tiffin Room.

uncovered a second ceiling above the Writers Bar and the Tiffin Room. This decorated ceiling is embellished with teeth-like patterns that is known as dentil moulding. All these new discoveries add even more layers to the history of this storied hotel. The fact that I am also part of this tale, in its lived history, is a privilege beyond words.

In order to share the history of Raffles Hotel Singapore with more guests, many of its key milestones and many of my favourite stories have been immortalised in stone, as well as in a new set of historical trail markers for self-guided tours. Stories from the past form a big part of my working day as the hotel's resident historian. But the future is something I look at with interest too, more so when I see in them in echoes of days gone by.

Take, for instance, the hotel's new restaurants. In many ways it has come full circle. In the early days, Raffles Hotel Singapore—the first hotel to hire a French chef—was known for pioneering culinary innovation. Today it counts not one, but two acclaimed restaurants under its roof: BBR by Alain Ducasse and La Dame de Pic, in keeping with its acclaimed reputation as a dining destination.

BBR by Alain Ducasse.

Writers Bar.

Tiffin Room.

Tradition continues in the form of the Tiffin Room and the Writers Bar. The latter is a nod to the many famous authors who have been a visitor or resident at Raffles Hotel Singapore since Joseph Conrad in 1888. The Tiffin Room, which has been part of the hotel since 1892, will go on serving North Indian food in vintage-styled tiffin boxes. History literally forms the foundations of this dining room as its wooden floorboards, dating from the early 1900s, have been reinstated.

And perhaps the best-known stalwart of the hotel, the Long Bar, continues its long reign. Home of the Singapore Sling, the historic bar is yet again "the place" to sip the pretty pink gin cocktail while revelling in the freedom to scatter peanut shells onto the floor (the only place in Singapore where it is perfectly fine to litter).

Long Bar.

Singapore Slings, the Long Bar's signature drink.

Grand Lobby.

Palm Court View.

It is yet another chapter to her long and lively story and ensures that this celebrated building will continue to bear witness to the flow of human history and be part of the Singapore Story. I am happy to do my part in continuing to share her stories. This book is just another way of paying homage to this Singapore institution. A love letter, if you will, to an icon that symbolises the human spirit of entrepreneurship, reinvention, and the constant striving to be better each day.

Colonnade Walkway.

14

ODE TO RAFFLES
HOTEL SINGAPORE

In 2019, Raffles Hotel Singapore turned 132
The Grand Dame of Beach Road into her
next phase of rebirth she had come.
Since the first restoration to the glory of 1915,
It was again time for reinvention and rise to fresh things,
A second restoration sees her renewed once more
With new interiors and modern updates
complementing traditions of yore.
Kipling's "Feed at the Raffles" will continue to stand the test
As fine dining, lavish meals and local delights
are served by renowned celebrity chefs.
Yet, Raffles did humbly begin in a ten-room bungalow,
From which this hotel's fame and size continue to grow and grow.

For a century it has hosted the best and brightest across the land.
From Somerset Maugham, John Wayne,
Michael Jackson and the Queen of England.
Fantastic tales abound of tiger hunts, boar chases and parties galore
(There were even fancy dress parties and
roller skating on the marble floors!)
It is the birthplace of the potent sweet mix of tropical fruit and gin
And the Long Bar is the place to go for this Singapore Sling
To Raffles Hotel Singapore let there always be style, elegance and charm
An enduring icon through the ages ever deserving of admiration
History has lived through and gone on around her,
but in her equanimous best,
Raffles Hotel Singapore has stood through the flow of change
and time's ongoing test.

I was honoured to receive the Long Service Award from General Manager Mr Christian Westbeld in 2019.

Back row from left to right: Myself, Theresa (wife), Anthony (son-in-law), Lissa and Laurene (daughters) and Jakki; Front row: Tyler and Kean (grandsons).

ACKNOWLEDGEMENTS

I would like to express my sincerest gratitude to Raffles Hotel Singapore, where I have been working for the past 48 years. It has given me invaluable insight into the hotel industry. Over the years, I have seen it all—I have worked under different management styles (8 out of the 12 general managers to be exact) and experienced the challenges of dealing with antiquated equipment. My time at the hotel has also given me many opportunities to meet famous personalities, among the most memorable was the Queen of England.

Raffles Hotel Singapore has provided me a lifetime of wonderful experiences, indeed.

ABOUT
THE AUTHOR

Leslie Basil Danker, resident historian, is a walking encyclopaedia of Raffles Hotel Singapore, a result of his keen interest in learning about the landmark building and its historical beginnings. Since joining Raffles in 1972, Mr Danker has taken the initiative to collect and painstakingly organise old press releases and photos of the hotel while continuing to delve into its role in Singapore's history.

On his morning walkabouts to meet and greet guests, Mr Danker freely shares his knowledge so as to give the Raffles residents a sense of the building's heritage. Today, Mr Danker remains the one person whom his colleagues rely upon for information whenever queries arise about the hotel's roots, from the residents, visitors or media.

During the restoration, he held the position of site supervisor working closely with engineers, architects and interior designers to

oversee the entire restoration process of the hotel. He was later promoted to guest relations manager. His immense knowledge and keen ability to apply new skills to his job have made Mr Danker a valuable and reliable member of the Raffles team.

Mr Danker's personal philosophy to his own learning journey is summed up in one of his favourite quotes from T.S. Eliot: "We shall never cease from exploration. At the end of all our exploring will be to arrive where we started and to know the place for the first time." For Mr Danker, it will be personally satisfying if he can continue to play his part in the growth of Raffles Hotel Singapore by helping to train his colleagues in the service standards and history of the hotel.